Turbulent Planet

White-Out
Blizzards

Claire Watts

Raintree

Chicago, Illinois

For information, address the publisher:
Raintree, 100 N. LaSalle, Suite 1200, Chicago, IL 60602

Printed and bound in China
Color Reproduction by Dot Gradations Ltd, UK
10 09 08 07 06
10 9 8 7 6 5 4 3 2 1

Library of Congress Cataloging-in-Publication Data

Watts, Claire.
  Whiteout blizzards / Claire Watts.
    p. cm. -- (Turbulent planet)
  Rev. ed. of: White-out : blizzards. 2005.
  Includes bibliographical references and index.
  ISBN 1-4109-1739-8 (library binding-hardcover) -- ISBN 1-4109-
1749-5 (pbk.) 1. Blizzards--Juvenile literature. I. Watts, Claire.
White-out. II. Title. III. Series.
  QC926.37.W38 2005b
  551.55'5--dc22
                                   2005008211

This leveled text is a version of Freestyle: Turbulent Planet:
White-out.

Acknowledgments
p.4/5, Corbis/Benjamin Lowy; p.5 top, Science Photo
Library/Micheal Marten; p.5 middle, Corbis Sygma/*The Scotsman*;
p.5 bottom, Science Photo Library/Alan & Sandy Carey; p.6/7,
Corbis/Warren Morgan; p.6 Corbis/Kevin Fleming; p.8/9,
Corbis/Randy Faris; p.8, Corbis/Jim Zuckerman; p.10/11,
Corbis/Richard Hamilton Smith; p.10, Science Photo Library/Dr
Juan Alean; p.11 Science Photo Library/W Bacon; p.12, Frank
Lane Picture Agency; p.13, Photodisc; p.13 right, Corbis/Niall
Benvie; p.14, Premium Stock; p.14 left, Corbis/Steve Terrill; p.15
Corbis/Bill Ross; p.16/17, Corbis/Doug Wilson; p.16,
Corbis/Christopher J Morris; p.17, Corbis/Brooks Kraft; p.18/19,
Corbis/Bettmann; p.18, Corbis/Karl Weatherly; p.19,
Corbis/Bettmann; p.20/21 Corbis/James L Amos; p.20,
Corbis/David Pollack; p.21, Corbis/Chuck Keeler Jr; p.22/23,
Corbis/Reinhard Eisle; p.22, Corbis/John Noble; p.23, Corbis/Julie
Habel; p.24, Science Photo Library/ Philippe Psaila; p.25,
Corbis/Julie Habel; p.26/27, Corbis/ Ecoscene/Nick Hawkes; p.26,
Science Photo Library/David Ducross; p.27, Science Photo
Library/Micheal Marten; p.28/29, Corbis/Micheal Boys; p.28,
Discovery Picture Library; p.29, Corbis/Paul Almasy; p.30/31,
Discovery Picture Library; p.30, Corbis/James Leynse; p.31,
Corbis/ Jack Fields; p.32, Galen Rowell; p.32 left, Galen Rowell;
p.33, Corbis Sygma/*The Scotsman*; p.33 right, Corbis/Peter
Harholdt; p.34/35, Corbis/Wolfgang Kaehler; p.34, Corbis/ Lowell
Georgia; p.36/37 Corbis Sygma/Tiroler Tageszeitung/Thomas
Boehm; p.36, Frank Lane Picture Agency/Jim Reed; p.37,
Corbis/Doug Wilson; p.38, Frank Lane Picture Agency/Jim Reed;
p.39, Corbis/Lowell Georgia; p.39 right, Linpac Environmental
Ltd; p.40/41, Corbis/Picimpact; p.40, Science Photo Library/Mark
Clarke; p.41, Science Photo Library/Alan & Sandy Carey; p.42/43,
Frank Lane Picture Agency/Jim Reed; p.42, Science Photo Library/
David Vaughan; p.43, Science Photo Library/Micheal Marten

Cover photograph reproduced with permission of Camera Press.

Every effort has been made to contact copyright holders of any
material reproduced in this book. Any omissions will be rectified
in subsequent printings if notice is given to the publishers.

Contents

Any words appearing in the text in bold, **like this,** are explained in the Glossary. You can also look out for some of them in the "Stormy Words" box at the bottom of each page.

Surrounded by Snow

Dark sky

Imagine you are walking in the street on a winter afternoon. You see dark clouds overhead. The **temperature** drops quickly, and snowflakes start to fall. The sky gets darker. The snow falls faster.

A cold wind starts blowing the snow across your face. Soon you can't even see where you are going. You have been caught in a blizzard.

Snow and wind

A blizzard is not just a heavy fall of snow. It is when snow falls and is also blown around by a strong wind.

White-Out

A very heavy blizzard is called a **white-out**. If you get caught in a white-out, you are surrounded by snow and can see nothing. White-outs are very dangerous. People can get lost or buried in **snowdrifts**.

Find out later . . .

. . . what kind of clouds bring heavy snow.

. . . what clothing is best for blizzards.

. . . how dogs can help people lost in snow.

snowdrift   deep bank of snow that has been piled up by the wind

What is a Blizzard?

Snowrollers

When wind blows snow along the ground, the snow can form into a snowball, like the ones these children made. Snowballs formed by the wind are called "snowrollers." They can be as big as 5 feet (1.5 meters) across.

A kind of snowstorm

A blizzard is a kind of **snowstorm**. It takes a heavy fall of snow and a fierce wind to produce a blizzard. A blizzard happens when the wind is blowing faster than 35 miles (56 kilometers) per hour. The **temperature** must be 20 °F (-7 °C) or lower.

In a blizzard **visibility** is less than 0.25 miles (0.4 kilometers). A blizzard lasts for at least three hours.

△ On Mount Everest in Nepal, the wind causes clouds of blowing snow.

High and dry

Blizzards usually occur in the middle of large, northern **continents**. They often happen in the mountains. In these areas, the air is dry and winter temperatures are low. Cold, dry air is perfect for blizzards.

Map

This map shows places mentioned in the text. It also shows places where blizzards happen most often.

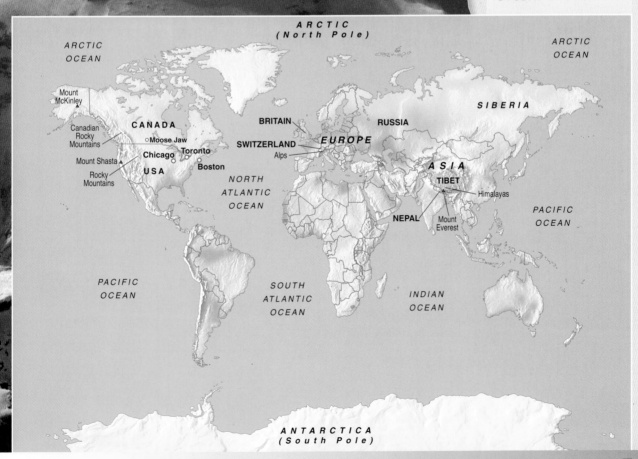

ARCTIC
(North Pole)

ARCTIC
OCEAN

ARCTIC
OCEAN

Mount
McKinley

Canadian
Rocky
Mountains

CANADA

Moose Jaw

BRITAIN

RUSSIA

SIBERIA

Mount Shasta

Chicago

Toronto

EUROPE

SWITZERLAND

Alps

Rocky
Mountains

USA

Boston

ASIA

TIBET

Himalayas

NORTH
ATLANTIC
OCEAN

NEPAL

Mount
Everest

PACIFIC
OCEAN

PACIFIC
OCEAN

SOUTH
ATLANTIC
OCEAN

INDIAN
OCEAN

ANTARCTICA
(South Pole)

continent   one of seven huge land areas on Earth

How snow is made

Clouds are made up of air and tiny drops of water. If the water drops **freeze**, they form **ice crystals**. The ice crystals can stick together and grow into snowflakes. When snowflakes get too heavy to stay in the air, they fall to the ground.

Snowflakes
Many snowflakes have six sides or points.

Sometimes, blizzards happen even when snow is not falling. Strong winds can lift fallen snow up into the air and blow it around. ▽

freeze   harden through loss of heat. Water freezes at 32 °F (0 °C).

Wet snow

When there is a lot of water in the air, larger snowflakes are formed. This kind of snow is called "wet snow." Wet snow is heavy and doesn't blow around so much in the wind.

Dry snow

When the air gets very cold, it contains less water. The snowflakes stay much smaller. This type of snow is light and powdery, and we call it "dry snow." It blows around easily. It is the kind of snow found in a blizzard.

Beautiful shapes

Some snowflakes are beautiful star shapes. Others are in the shape of columns or blocks. Below are some snowflake shapes.

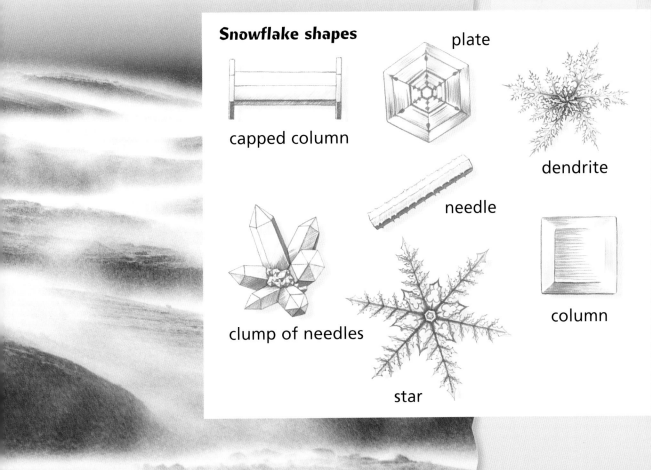

Snowflake shapes

capped column

plate

dendrite

needle

clump of needles

column

star

ice crystal   piece of ice with parts and surfaces arranged in a regular pattern

Shaping the snow

When snow gets blown around, it seems to change the shape of the landscape. The actual shape of the land underneath is hidden. The wind can make amazing shapes and patterns with snow.

Making shapes

Sometimes the wind blows the snow into an overhanging ledge called a **cornice**.

Snowdrifts

The wind can also make **snowdrifts**. Snowdrifts form when the wind blows snow into a big pile. The wind can pack the snow down hard.

snowdrift   deep bank of snow that has been piled up by the wind

Snowdrifts can get so thick that they become difficult to dig out after a blizzard.

Alaskan avalanche

When deep snowdrifts form on a mountain, there is a danger of an **avalanche**. Avalanches happen when large areas of snow suddenly break away and slide down a mountain. They can sweep people away and bury whole buildings.

Alaskan avalanche
This photo shows an avalanche tumbling down Mount McKinley in Alaska.

The wind has swept this snow into a pattern like waves.
▽

avalanche   falling mass of snow, ice, rocks, or mud

Blizzards in the Wild

Keeping close

These emperor penguin chicks are in **Antarctica**, where it is very cold. They stay close together to keep warm. Their fluffy feathers help keep heat in.

Coping with cold

Many blizzards happen in areas where there are few people. In these wild places, animals and other living things have learned to cope with snow, wind, and cold.

Adaptable animals

Animals and birds have several ways of **adapting** to blizzards and other cold conditions. Some grow thick fur and feathers. Others huddle together for warmth. Many animals store food for the winter.

Hibernation

Some animals, including insects, make nests and **hibernate** when it gets cold. They stay in their nests and sleep until the weather gets warmer.

◁ This porcupine's long hair helps keep it warm

Winter stores
Red squirrels bury nuts and other food in the fall. When winter comes, they can use the stored food to live on.

hibernate   spend the winter in a deep sleep or state of rest

Close to the ground

Trees and smaller plants also **adapt** to blizzards and cold weather. In places with heavy snow and wind, many plants grow close to the ground. Their short stems don't break so easily in the wind and snow.

Protected plants

Snow blankets the ground in winter and can protect plants. Below, irises have grown through the snow from bulbs in the soil beneath.

△ Snow has completely covered these fir trees in the state of Washington.

Bending branches

In high, cold regions, most trees are **evergreens**. Their branches are springy. They hold the snow's heavy weight. The branches will also bend instead of breaking in strong winds.

Tough leaves

Trees **absorb** water from the ground through their roots. When the water in the ground **freezes** in winter, trees have no source of water. Evergreen trees have tough, waxy leaves that lose very little water. The leaves help keep moisture in the tree.

Mount Shasta

The largest **snowstorm** ever recorded was at Mount Shasta, California (above), in 1959. In that storm, 189 inches (480 centimeters) of snow fell.

evergreen   trees that keep their leaves all year round

The Blizzard Strikes

Power down

Blizzards can damage power lines and cut off the electricity supply to homes. People are without heat and light until the power company can fix the lines.

Getting around

Blizzards can cause all kinds of problems in **populated** areas. Fast-falling snow makes it difficult to see. **Visibility** is very poor.

Standstill

Airplanes cannot fly safely in heavy snow. Airports close when there is a blizzard. Schools and workplaces close, too, so that people will not have to travel in dangerous conditions.

visibility   distance it is possible to see

No services

Sometimes blizzards bring down **power lines** and telephone cables. Power **outages** leave people without electricity just when they need it most. If snow blocks the roads, delivery trucks cannot get to stores and gas stations. Supplies of food and gas can run out quickly.

Grounded
Below, **snowplows** try to clear the runway at a Boston airport during a **snowstorm**. Airplanes have to stay on the ground until the weather improves.

△ Blizzards cause bad visibility and slippery roads. Road travel can be very dangerous.

Blizzard hazards

Heavy **snowstorms** are very dangerous for people who are caught outside. It is easy to get lost when **visibility** is bad.

Stuck in the snow

Walking through deep snow is very tiring. People can collapse from **exhaustion**. They can fall into a **snowdrift** or other deep snow. Sometimes it can be impossible to get out.

Snow blind

The **glare** from snow can cause snow blindness. People who are outside in snow should wear goggles or sunglasses.

German soldiers ▷ huddle together in Russia during World War II. Many did not survive the cold winter.

exhaustion extreme tiredness

Hypothermia

Most of all the cold **temperatures** are a danger. When a person's body temperature drops, he or she can develop **hypothermia**. Breathing and blood flow slow down. People stop moving, and they cannot think clearly. Hypothermia can kill people if they are not rescued from the cold.

Fatal expedition

The five men below were members of the second expedition to reach the **South Pole**. They got there on January 17, 1912. On its return journey, the team was hit by terrible blizzards. All five men died.

hypothermia   condition in which a person's body gets too cold to survive for long

This truck slid off the road into heavy snow. ▽

What to do

If your car gets stuck in a blizzard:

- Stay in the car.
- Tie a bright-colored cloth to the antenna or mirror.
- Start the car and use the heater for twenty minutes every hour.
- Keep the exhaust pipe clear of snow.
- Keep one car window slightly open.
- Move your arms and legs.

Out on the road

One of the most dangerous places to be in a blizzard is on the road in a vehicle. Even when a storm is just beginning, it is safer to stay home.

Slipping and skidding

Roads are very slippery when they are covered in just a thin layer of snow. Cars and trucks without **four-wheel drive** can easily **skid**.

four-wheel drive having an engine that turns all four wheels

Stranded

As a storm gets heavier, vehicles can get stuck when their tires sink in the soft snow. Drivers can be **stranded** far from any shelter.

Moving slowly
Vehicles must move very slowly in blizzards. Driving slowly can save lives on busy highways like the one below.

Hidden dangers

Deep or **drifting** snow can hide dangers on the road, such as rocks or fallen trees. Falling snow makes it hard to see the way. Snow also hides markings that show drivers where they are and help keep them on the road.

stranded   stuck in a difficult place without help   21

On the farm

Most animals are better prepared than people for winter. It can still be hard for them to survive a blizzard. Snow covers the grass that **livestock** eat, and their drinking water can **freeze** over.

Huddling together

Herds of animals often stand close together to share their body heat. They take turns being on the cold, outside edges of the group.

Winter grazing
These sheep have found a patch of grass under the snow.

Seeking shelter

Farm animals often seek shelter from a blizzard against a fence or wall. If the snow builds up into a **snowdrift** where they are sheltering, the animals may get buried and freeze to death.

Snow caves

Sometimes, the snow can actually help animals survive. When snow covers a sheep, the sheep's body heat can melt the snow. The snow around the sheep forms a cave and keeps it warm.

Warm wool

People do not have **fleece** to keep them warm, as sheep do. But they can protect themselves from snow with wool scarves and hoods.

◁ Cattle look for food and shelter during blizzards.

fleece   woolly coat of a sheep or other animal

Predicting Blizzards

Being prepared

It is very important to be prepared for blizzards. Weather scientists, called **meteorologists**, watch out for signs of blizzards and other bad weather. They warn people of dangers on the way.

Weather warnings

Winter weather warnings are **broadcast** on television and radio, and displayed on the Internet. The warnings are put out by the National Weather Service.

◁ A meteorologist is taking measurements of the snowfall.

Warning	Snowfall	Wind	Visibility
Heavy snow	More than 4 in. (10 cm)	Less than 32 miles (51 km) per hour	More than 0.25 miles (0.4 km)
Drifting snow or blizzards	Heavy snowfall and/or blowing snow	Over 35 miles (56 km) per hour	0.25 miles (0.4 km) or less
Very heavy snow or severe blizzards	More than 6 in. (15 cm)	Over 45 miles (72 km) per hour	Near zero

Watching developments

It is hard to **predict** exactly what the weather will do. If meteorologists think severe winter weather is coming, the National Weather Service will issue a general winter storm warning. The scientists will then see what conditions develop. Next, they will put out heavy snow warnings, or blizzard warnings if they need to.

It is important to pay attention to weather warnings. When people ignore warnings, they can get **stranded** in the snow. ▽

Weather stations

Meteorologists use **weather stations** to help them **predict** weather patterns. Weather stations record information about **temperatures**, wind speed, and **air pressure**.

Satellites

Up in space, weather **satellites** also record weather information. They send pictures to Earth of clouds, winds, and other features. The images help meteorologists to see which areas may soon be hit with severe weather.

Satellite

This is a drawing of a weather satellite. It sends information back to Earth every 30 minutes.

This weather station is ▷ in an open place. Areas with no buildings or trees are best for weather stations.

air pressure   force of air pressing down on Earth

△ Cumulonimbus clouds are big and heavy. They often bring heavy snowfall.

weather station   place where observations about the weather are recorded

Preparing for Winter

Storm supplies

These are good things to have in a blizzard:

- first-aid kit
- battery-powered radio
- candles
- camping stove and fuel
- matches
- canned food
- can opener
- flashlight

- bottled water
- warm clothes and blankets.

Protecting homes

At the start of winter, people get ready for blizzard season. They make sure their homes are **insulated** to keep them warm. Protecting water pipes is very important. When water **freezes**, it **expands** and can burst pipes.

If a blizzard hits, people may be snowed in for a long time. They need to make sure they have plenty of supplies.

Fruit and vegetables △ that have been bottled will keep through winter.

Stocking up

In the past, there were no **snowplows**. People living in the country sometimes had to wait until the snow melted to get fresh supplies. Sometimes they had to wait until spring before they could reach a nearby town.

Today people don't get snowed in for months. Still preparing for a blizzard means thinking ahead. The most important supplies are enough food, water, and **fuel** to last several days.

Built for snow

This building in Switzerland is always ready for snow. Its overhanging roof helps snow slide off without blocking doors and windows.

Preparing the roads

When a blizzard is **forecast**, trucks are sent out to spread gravel and salt on the roads. The salt melts the snow when it hits the ground. The gravel helps car tires grip on a slippery road.

Buried

In 1996 a blizzard in New York dropped over 22 inches (56 centimeters) of snow. **Snowplows** cleared the street, but parked cars were buried. This woman is starting to dig her car out after the storm.

forecast   use information to work out ahead of time what the weather will do

Just in case

In places where there is a lot of snow, drivers get their cars ready for winter. They keep the gas tank filled up. Many people also store some emergency supplies in their vehicle, in case they get stuck. They carry shovels, food, boots, and blankets.

Winter wheels

Snow tires and **snow chains** make driving much safer in winter. They help the wheels grip the road when it is slippery.

◁   A truck spreads gravel and salt on the roads.

Putting on chains

These men are fitting snow chains to the tires of their truck. The chains will help them drive through deep snow.

snow chains   chains attached to tires to help grip the road

Protecting Yourself

Keeping warm

It is very important to protect yourself from the cold. Wearing warm clothes is the best way to do this. Several layers of thin clothing are better than one thick layer. The layers trap warm air next to the skin.

Frostbite

If parts of your body **freeze**, you can get frostbite. The body part gets numb, and the skin turns white. Then it gets red and swollen. Eventually, dark blisters appear.

The Inuit people

Inuit people who live in the **Arctic** wear loose coats made of **caribou** fur. The coats are easy to move around in, and they keep warm air in.

Inuit people keep warm in traditional fur clothing. ▽

caribou   large deer that lives in the Arctic and northern North America

From head to toe

Most body heat is lost through the head, hands, and feet. If you are in a blizzard or other very cold weather, you need to keep these parts warm. Good hats, gloves, and boots can stop you from getting **frostbite**.

This mountain rescue team dresses in bright colors and waterproof clothing.
▽

Snow goggles

The Inuit used to make goggles from bark or bone. Narrow slits in the goggles allowed the person to see, but they reduced **glare** from the snow.

Inuit   people native to northern North America and Greenland

Finding shelter

If you get caught in a blizzard, you must find shelter quickly. If there are no buildings around, you need to find a place that protects you from the wind. Look for a natural shelter, such as a wall or cave.

Make sure your shelter is in a safe place. Avoid places with a danger of **snowdrifts** and falling snow.

Drifted in

People must choose shelters carefully. Snowdrifts, like the one above, can block doors and trap people inside buildings.

This person is building an igloo. A skilled △ builder can build an igloo in about an hour.

Building a shelter

Sometimes, your only choice is to build a shelter from the snow itself. In the **Arctic**, the **Inuit** make **igloos**. They cut blocks of firm snow and build dome-shaped shelters.

On mountains climbers caught in a sudden blizzard dig into the snow to make themselves a snow hole, or cave. In igloos and snow holes, it is important to leave a hole to let air in.

How to make a snow hole

Below is a diagram showing a typical snow hole. It is important to make an air hole if you seal the entrance.

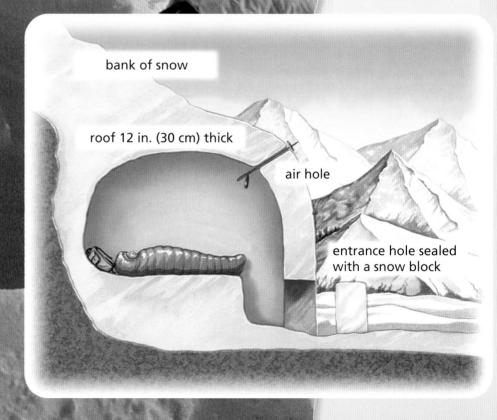

bank of snow

roof 12 in. (30 cm) thick

air hole

entrance hole sealed with a snow block

---

igloo   dome-shaped shelter made from snow blocks

After the Storm

Going outside

After a blizzard is over, people begin to go outside again. Sometimes, they have to dig themselves out. Shoveling heavy snow is hard work.

Cut off

Sometimes, the snowfall has been so heavy that people cannot dig their way out. They are completely cut off by snow.

Isolation

Houses in remote areas can be cut off from the outside world during and after **snowstorms**.

△ A helicopter delivers food to a community cut off by snow.

isolated   cut off or hard to reach from other places

Air rescue

If people are **isolated** by snow, small airplanes can fly over and drop emergency supplies. Helicopters can land with crates of food in **remote** areas. They can also pick up people who need medical attention and transport them to the hospital.

Stuck

A **snowdrift** formed around this car during a snowstorm. It may be days before the snow melts enough to get the car out.

PREMIUM BANANAS
PRODUCT OF
COLOMBIA 14154

PREMIUM BANANAS
PRODUCT OF
COLOMBIA

remote   far away

Clearing roads

After a blizzard the roads have to be cleared. Shifting a **snowdrift** several feet thick takes a **heavy-duty** vehicle.

Plowing and blowing

Snowplows are sent out during and after blizzards to keep roads clear. As they travel snowplows shovel snow off the road and push it to the side. Machines called **snowblowers** are used, too. They work well when the snow is dry and powdery.

This snowplow scrapes the road clear
▽   of snow. It also releases gravel.

heavy-duty   able to perform tough tasks

A snowblower makes a path through deep snow. ▽

Spreading gravel

In snowy neighborhoods containers of gravel stand in the streets. People can spread the gravel on sidewalks to make them less slippery.

Highways first

Snowplows work on the biggest roads first. Highways with heavy traffic must be made safe. Smaller roads are cleared as soon as possible.

snowblower   machine that sucks in snow to remove it from a
path or road and then blows it out elsewhere

Out of nowhere

In the mountains a blizzard can appear out of nowhere. Skiers, hikers, and mountain climbers can suddenly find themselves lost in the snow.

Search and rescue

Even after the storm passes, people may be **stranded** or even buried in **snowdrifts** or **avalanches**. It is time to send out the search and rescue team.

Ambulance on skis

In ski areas emergency and medical workers use **snowmobiles** to rescue injured skiers.

Rescue workers

Search and rescue teams search for clues that will lead them to lost people. They use long poles to check for people buried in deep snow. They often have specially trained dogs that can **track** people with their sense of smell.

Search and rescue is urgent work. If people are left in the snow, they may die from **hypothermia**.

St. Bernards

St. Bernard dogs came from the Swiss Alps. Long ago they were trained to find lost travelers in the snowy mountains.

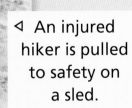

◁ An injured hiker is pulled to safety on a sled.

track   look for someone or something by following tracks or other clues, such as scent

41

Blizzard Survival Guide

Surviving a blizzard

The freezing snow and fierce wind that make a blizzard are a dangerous mix. People can die if they are not careful. If you are in a place where blizzards strike, make sure you are prepared. It may help you to survive.

Lifeline

At this camp in the **Arctic**, scientists have strung up a line of ropes. The line helps them find their way around camp in a blizzard.

If **power lines** go down, electrical △ power is cut off. You will need another source of heat and light.

  power line cable that carries electricity supply from a power plant to users

Things to remember

We have seen there are many ways to prepare for a blizzard and to protect yourself when it arrives:

- Check the weather **forecast**, and look for signs of bad weather.
- Stock up on food, heating **fuel**, and gas.
- Stay inside.
- Don't travel unless you really need to.
- Carry emergency supplies.
- Find shelter if you get caught outside.
- Beware of being trapped by **snowdrifts**.
- Wear layers, and keep your head covered.

Storm signs

Remember to look out for signs of coming storms. Dark clouds and cold **temperatures** tell you that snow may be on its way.

fuel   something that can be burned to produce heat

Find Out More

Organizations

The National Weather Service

This is an organization that keeps track of weather conditions around the country. The National Weather Service issues severe weather warnings when necessary. Contact them at the following address:

National Weather Service,
National Oceanic and Atmospheric Administration,
US Dept. of Commerce,
1325 East West Highway, Silver Spring, MD 20910

Books

Murphy, Jim. *Blizzard! The Storm That Changed America*. New York: Scholastic, 2000.

Scheff, Duncan. *Nature on the Rampage: Blizzards*. Chicago: Raintree, 2003.

Thomas, Rick and Denise Shea. *White-out! A Book about Blizzards (Amazing Science)*. Minneapolis: Picture Window Books, 2005.

World Wide Web

If you want to find out more about blizzards, you can search the Internet using keywords such as these:

- blizzard +news
- snow +disasters
- winter +safety

You can also find your own keywords by using headings or words from this book. Use the search tips on the next page to help you find the most useful websites.

Search tips

There are billions of pages on the Internet. It can be difficult to find exactly what you are looking for. These tips will help you find useful websites more quickly.

- Know what you want to find out.
- Use simple keywords.
- Use two to six keywords in a search.
- Only use names of people, places, or things.
- If your keywords are made up of two or more words that go together, put quote marks around them—for example "weather satellite."
- Use the + sign to join keywords together—for example weather +disaster.

Where to search

Search engine

A search engine looks through millions of website pages. It lists all the sites that match the words in the search box. You will find the best matches are at the top of the list, on the first page.

Search directory

A person instead of a computer has sorted a search directory. You can search by keyword or subject and browse through the different sites. It is like looking through books on a library shelf.

Glossary

absorb soak up

adapt change to suit conditions

air pressure force of air pressing down on Earth

Antarctica the continent around the South Pole

Arctic the region around the North Pole

avalanche falling mass of snow, ice, rocks, or mud

broadcast send out information by radio and television

caribou large deer that lives in the Arctic and northern North America

continent one of seven huge land areas on Earth

cornice overhanging ledge of snow

drifting being moved by wind

evergreen trees that keep their leaves all year round

exhaustion extreme tiredness

expand get bigger

fleece woolly coat of a sheep or other animal

forecast use information to work out ahead of time what the weather will do

four-wheel drive having an engine that turns all four wheels. Vehicles with four-wheel drive perform better in snow and on ice.

freeze harden through loss of heat. Water freezes at 32 °F (0 °C).

frostbite freezing of a part of the body, such as fingers, toes, ears, or nose

fuel something that can be burned to produce heat

glare harsh, bright light that is uncomfortable to look at

heavy-duty able to perform tough tasks

hibernate spend the winter in a deep sleep or state of rest

hypothermia condition in which a person's body gets too cold to survive for long

ice crystal piece of ice with parts and surfaces arranged in a regular pattern

igloo dome-shaped shelter made from snow blocks

insulate made so that warmth can be kept in

Inuit people native to northern North America and Greenland

isolated cut off or hard to reach from other places

livestock animals kept by people, such as cows, sheep, and horses

meteorologist scientist who studies the weather

outage period when electrical power fails or is interrupted

populated   lived in by people

power line   cable that carries electricity supply from a power plant to users

predict   say when something will happen

remote   far away

satellite   vehicle sent into space to travel around Earth

skid   slip sideways out of control

snowblower   machine that sucks in snow to remove it from a path or road and then blows it out elsewhere

snow chains   chains attached to tires to help grip the road

snowdrift   deep bank of snow that has been piled up by the wind

snowmobile   small vehicle that travels through snow on skis

snowplow   vehicle that clears snow from the road

snowstorm   heavy fall of snow

South Pole   most southern point of Earth

stranded   stuck in a difficult place without help

temperature   level of heat or coldness

track   look for someone or something by following tracks or other clues, such as scent

visibility   distance it is possible to see

weather station   place where observations about the weather are recorded

white-out   bad blizzard in which nothing but snow can be seen

Index